Barcelona to Brazil:

on Tour

with MANCHESTER UNITED

Barcelona to Brazil:  on Tour

with MANCHESTER UNITED

John Peters with Adam Bostock

Thanks to Alan Bray, the technician who reproduced all these images,
and to PCL in Manchester for their continued support.

First published in Great Britain in 2000 by Manchester United Books

an imprint of André Deutsch Limited
76 Dean Street
London W1V 5HA
www.vci.co.uk

10 9 8 7 6 5 4 3 2 1

A catalogue record for this book is available from the British Library

ISBN 0 233 99888 8

Additional interviews by Rebecca Tow
Cover and page design by DW Design, London
Printed and bound in Italy by Officine Grafiche DeAgostini

Contents

Introduction

I'm the first person to admit it. I'm a lucky man to be travelling the world with Manchester United, taking photographs everywhere – from Barcelona to Brazil. I think I must have bought a lucky rabbit's foot at some stage. Or maybe it's something to do with the number seven, which has been a significant number in my life. I had seven years in my first job – working for the Thomson News Group in Manchester – and seven years in my second, taking publicity photographs for Granada Television. I'm just wondering what will happen at the end of this season – my seventh at Manchester United!

I've actually been taking photos of footballers for much longer than that, starting not long after I left school with one O-level (in Commerce). During my years as a darkroom technician and all-round gopher at Thomson House, I met and started to work with several photographers in my spare time. One of them was a man named Peter Price, who would often ask me to cover Stoke City in the great days of Alan Hudson and Bolton Wanderers, when their current manager Sam Allardyce was still playing. I would take black and white photographs and sell them to national newspapers on Peter's behalf. It was a good start for me, but only that. The Thomson studios closed down in 1979, making me redundant at the age of twenty-one. It was then that I began a freelance career earning about forty pounds a week with a Nikon F1 camera that I bought for about seventy pounds. I had a lot of free time – I spent most afternoons on the driving range – but that changed with the news from my wife that I was to become a father. I realised I had to do a little more than practise my golf swing!

I returned to full-time work in the photographic department at Granada Television. It was a completely different form of photography. I found myself taking publicity shots of everything from *Coronation Street* to *The Comedians* for listings magazines and newspapers, or shooting locations and sets for production designers. Against everybody's advice, I resigned from Granada in 1987. At the age of twenty-nine, I was restless, and determined to get back into freelancing, rather than tie myself to an office every day from nine-thirty to six.

My aim as a freelancer was to work primarily within television and theatre, complemented by some PR projects. One day I might be photographing Laurence Olivier – he once threw me out of a studio

> **My favourite photos** of John's are the ones you don't know he's taking. I absolutely love them. I've got some fond and treasured memories through the photos that John has printed for me. I've been all over the world now, and I've got photos knocking about from Japan, Brazil and Australia. I never have to take my own camera, because John's always about, he's a professional and he takes some great photos.
>
> **albert morgan**

for annoying him; the next, I'd be in a new pub, taking pictures for the brewery of their happy, smiling bar staff.

I also worked for the Catholic newspaper, the *Universe*, and spent two Christmas mornings in Strangeways prison, photographing the Bishop of Salford as he conducted mass for the inmates. I was really enjoying my freelance work when I received a phone call from Paul Doherty, a good friend of mine from the Granada days when he was their head of sport. He told me Manchester United were looking for a photographer to do some work for their merchandising division, in particular the new club magazines.

My first assignment was to enter the United dressing room after the final match of the 1992/93 season and photograph the players with the Premier League trophy. They beat Blackburn on the night, and although it wasn't a crucial result, I'm glad they won. My job is so much easier when they're winning matches. My only concern was that nobody knew me. But looking back, nobody really cared, they were in such high spirits. It was just a case of, 'Hey you – take a picture of me with this cup.' I took around 200 colour photographs on the night, including a very special one of Sir Matt Busby, Alex Ferguson and the Premier League trophy. Sir Matt was the last United manager to win the Championship in 1967, and his expression in that photo is magical. You can see in his face that he was very proud of what Alex had achieved, by winning the title in 1993. That photo remains one of my favourites. United's merchandising team were also very pleased with the final prints from that historic evening. So pleased, in fact, that my next assignment came just a few days later, when the team paraded the Championship around the streets of Manchester for the first time in twenty-six years.

I joined the players on the open-topped bus and it was quite a challenge, bearing in mind that most photographers shoot the parades from a building, or on the street below. Actually being on the bus gives and demands a different angle. I had a few

problems, because the players tended to hold the cup out, showing it to the crowd. So I either had to get them to turn round, or I had to lean out and precariously balance myself on the edge of a moving bus! I managed to stay on the bus, though, and again the results were very pleasing. I was offered some more work by Manchester United, starting with a long trip to sunny South Africa on the first team's pre-season tour. I had to make a big decision, knowing that I'd be letting down some of my freelance clients if I boarded the plane. After discussions with my family, I decided it was an opportunity I couldn't miss. So I went to South Africa and spent ten days getting to know the players, including Roy Keane, who'd joined the club that summer. I had a great time, and again took some good photographs.

South Africa's climate, even in their winter, lends itself to photography. I took hundreds of pictures, I forget exactly how many now. When I came back to Manchester, there was talk of doing a book, based on that one trip. That didn't happen, but the photos appeared in the club magazines, and I was asked by United if I was prepared to work for them long-term, as the official club photographer. It was a dream offer, so obviously I said yes. I informed my other clients that I wouldn't be available as much, and so it began.

I've since covered every single first team game, home and away, including pre-season friendlies and testimonials for the last seven years. That's an awful lot of games, and some of them are just a blur now. But far from being jaded, I still get excited about every single game. There's always something different to photograph. There's been an amazing turnover of players in seven years, for example – only a handful still remain from that first trip to South Africa.

As you'll see in this book, Manchester United are a well-travelled football club, and that's wonderful for me. Each location offers a new backdrop, especially in Europe or further afield. In this collection you'll find a great variety of pictures, from Jaap Stam dancing in Barcelona to Dwight Yorke snoozing on a private jet to Turin. Of course, the key to my taking photographs of these off-duty moments is my invisible 'access all areas' pass. For that I'm very grateful to the players, with whom I have a good relationship. It's based on trust and honesty, of course – the players know I won't take any pictures that portray them in the wrong light. So if the club magazine, for example,

asks me to photograph a player in a certain style, I'll say no if the player says no. It's as simple as that.

At all times, I have to be mindful of the privileged position I'm in. The players are allowing me time and access to a part of their lives that would normally be very private. So too is the Boss, Sir Alex Ferguson. He's ultimately the most important person with regard to my player access. I can sometimes tell, just by looking at him, whether or not it's a good opportunity to ask for permission to photograph something. There are times when I'll walk away and leave it for another day.

I remember one occasion when I seemed to be taking the wrong picture at the wrong time. I'd been asked by the club to take a photograph for the annual report of three new signings, who at the time were Jaap Stam, Dwight Yorke and Jesper Blomqvist.

I agreed with the players to take the photo at a training session in Munich, where they were preparing for a big Champions League game against Bayern. So I gathered them together, and they were just putting their arms around each other when the Boss shouted, 'John! You're not on holiday now.' He obviously thought I was taking a happy snap for the players, but he was fine when I explained what the photograph was really for. I only wish I'd explained it to him before... being shouted at by Sir Alex Ferguson is not a nice feeling, and should never be encouraged! I'm fully aware that he can deny me access at any time, so I bother him as little as possible. After all, the Boss has got something to do that is a lot more important than pose for photographs – win football matches! But he understands that photography and the media in general represent a huge part of Manchester United and its future.

Nearly all of the departments at Old Trafford need and use photographs, be it for a cheque presentation, a team poster for the Megastore, or an action shot for the club media.

> " I find it a real benefit to have John around. Often when we come back from a trip, he'll give us a few photographs. Without him, I'd go through life, travelling to these tours and games without any souvenirs or pictures to remember them by. "
>
> **steve mcclaren**

The club media has certainly grown in my seven seasons, and I've taken photographs for all of the various arms – MUTV, www.manutd.com, *Manchester United* and *Glory Glory Man United* magazines, the matchday programme, even Manchester United Radio, to adorn their studio walls.

There are other, non-commercial uses. This season, for example, I photographed every member of the staff with the four trophies – the Premiership, the European Cup, the FA Cup and the Intercontinental-Cup. The club's management felt it was something that may never be repeated again, and I think it was a very generous gesture on their part. Photographs like that will never be seen by Joe Public, of course. They don't end up on a T-shirt or a calendar, making money for Manchester United. But it's the sort of photography that can be requested of me, week in week out.

The demands of the job can make the hours unsociable, and they sometimes keep me away from home for hours on end. I owe an awful lot of thanks to my family. My mum and dad have always been supportive, especially in the early days, when they let me do what I wanted to do. My wife, my son and my daughter have always given their continuous support. I've always talked things through with them, to keep them in the picture as to where my career is going. My son Matthew is now working with me and we travel together to away games – I appreciate his company.

I'd also like to thank the players, and the Boss. Without their permission, I wouldn't have been able to capture the images and moments you'll see in the book. Last but not least, my good friend Paul Doherty for the initial introduction to Manchester United. Had it not been for his phone call in May 1993... well, you wouldn't be reading these words.

I hope you enjoy it, this insider look at United on the move, from Barcelona to Brazil.

" I think John's different because he's around the club all the time. He's here two or three times a week. The players and the manager have got used to him, and I'm sure a lot of the fans recognize him. It's important that you trust someone who's taking photos of you, and all the lads do. That's why the relationship is good between the players and John. "

david beckham

John Peters
Official Club Photographer
Manchester United PLC

Chapter 1

Barcelona

Manchester United's Treble dreams came true on a magical night in Barcelona. Wednesday 26 May 1999 is a date that forever will be etched in the memories of the players, staff and supporters, not to mention the club photographer who felt privileged to capture the evening's events on film.

I first pressed the shutter on the day of the European Cup Final around eleven o'clock in the morning when the players left their hotel for a short stroll. I stopped taking photographs at around half past six the following morning, when the celebrations following United's momentous 2-1 victory began to die down. I couldn't tell you how many rolls of film I used that night, but I guess I would have used only five per cent of them had United lost the match! The party was certainly a busy event for me, as I moved around the room, photographing the players dancing away and deservedly having a wonderful night with their girlfriends or wives, friends and relatives. I probably lost a stone in weight in the process!

The photographs you'll see in this chapter are very special to me. I was aware that the party was very private, so I thank the players for allowing me to publish these photographs, some of which show a personal side to their lives. Of course, we came so close to a very different kind of evening in Barcelona. I had been forced by the stewards, because there were so many photographers, to spend the first half of the Final at the wrong end of the field, feeling physically sick as I photographed Bayern Munich's attack, including their early goal by Mario Basler.

In the second half, when time was running out, I was concentrating on what photographs needed to be taken to record a very sad event, a defeat in the European Cup Final. Then Teddy Sheringham equalized. I then tried to work out where I'd position myself for extra-time, when the players would change ends again. But while that was still in my mind, Ole Gunnar Solskjaer scored what turned out to be the winning goal.

Suddenly goose bumps appeared all over me, and I screamed! When the final whistle went, I raced the other photographers to the centre of the field, still screaming. So began an unbelievable night in Barcelona, and the perfect chapter to open this book with.

John Peters

> "This is a special photograph because we all came through together, and it's a way of saying thank you to Eric Harrison because we realize how important he has been to our lives and careers."
>
> *gary neville*

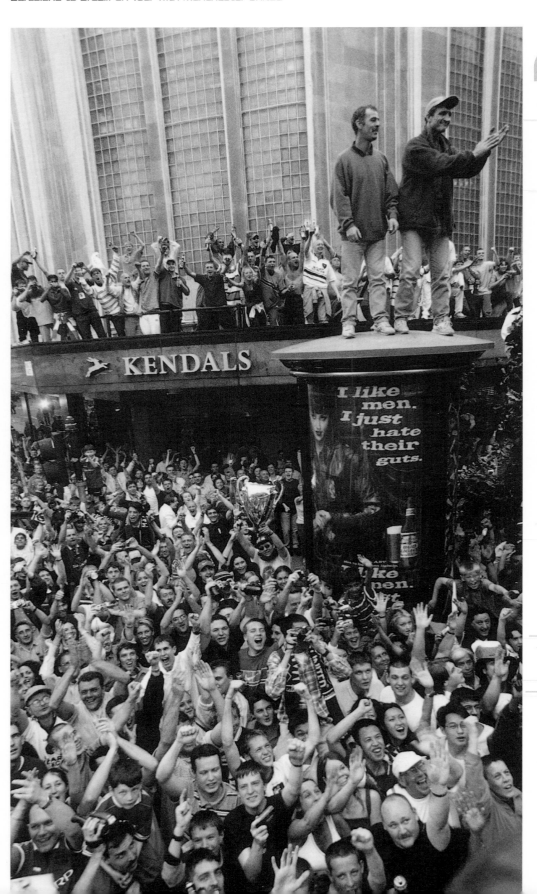

KENDALS

I like
men.
I just
hate
their
guts.

" **The homecoming parade** was a fantastic occasion. In this photograph I was probably thinking about the sheer amount of people that had come to see us, the crowd was amazing. "

gary neville

" **I'd be surprised if we'll** see pictures like this again. The fans climbed and clambered on to every building, bus stop or lamp post to get a view of the team bus as it passed by. It really was a breathtaking sight from the bus, looking out, in particular on Deansgate in the city centre. There was a continuous, high-volume roar as we moved along the parade route. "

 john peters

"That was a great day, just after we'd won the European Cup. I don't think I can get a buzz like that again in my career. Winning the Treble and then coming back to such a homecoming – it was a great feeling."

andy cole

 ❝ This was the players' view as we
approached the beginning of Deansgate –
the backsides of several police horses! ❞

⇑ **john peters**

" **As you can see I gate-crashed this photo**
taken at the aftermatch party. At first, I didn't see Ryan,
so I thought it was a shot of all the England lads together.
'What about me?' I said. 'Why can't I be in it?'
Then I realized it was all the young players who'd come
through the United ranks together.
They didn't want to hurt my feelings, so I just said, 'Look,
I'm in this anyway. You can't leave me out.'
I'm glad I made the photo – me as one of the young lads! "

↑ **teddy sheringham**

"Me and Nicky on the
night of Barcelona,
never wanting to put
the cup down."

← *paul scholes*

> " **My dad's mate Macca**
> entertaining the lads
> with his jig of joy. "
>
> **paul scholes** $\Rightarrow$

> " **I'd call this one**
> Me and My Baby.
> It was that night anyway.
> We had two great nights after
> winning the League and the
> FA Cup Final. But when we
> won the Treble, it was the night
> of all nights. "
>
> $\Leftarrow$ **teddy sheringham**

> ## Me and My Baby again!
> It was an unbelievable night.
> As you can see, we were having
> a great time! I'm not sure
> what time this was,
> but the party went on until
> the early hours. I think I went to
> bed at about six.

teddy sheringham ⇒

"On nights of celebration, Ryan has become famous for his Elvis Presley dance. Magic photo!"

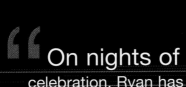 →

 "It was late in the morning, and they were playing songs about each player on the speaker system. My song came on, so I had to do something on the dancefloor for my minute of fame. I would rather have danced with my girlfriend, but still, that night was very special. The season was over, we'd won everything and everyone felt relaxed and so happy. "

⇑ **ole gunnar solskjaer**

"This was taken towards the end of the party. David May was treating us to his impression of Frank Sinatra, singing United songs. I think someone turned his microphone off eventually! "

john peters ⇨

> **This is a nice shot,** taken after the game in Barcelona. Of course, we had a couple of drinks, and I think Peter has a cigar in his mouth. This was probably about four o'clock in the morning. **jaap stam**

The first thing I remember about this

incident was someone coming up behind me and taking
my glasses off in the dressing room after the
Champions League Final in May 1999. I think it was Jimmy Curran,
who's not in the picture. Then my legs went,
there was a load of laughing and it was 'in we go boys!'
It was a waste of time struggling. I was just celebrating at the time,
jumping up and down, ecstatic like everyone else in the dressing room.
The next minute, the lads decided Albert had to go
in the jacuzzi pool so Albert went in! I think I grabbed David Fevre
by the neck and he just followed me in.
The only thing I was grateful for was that I didn't bang my
head on the side! Keano's there, ready to pour
the champagne over my head and there's David
holding me under.
I came out with a good expression
on my face as the last photograph shows!
It was a brilliant night in Barcelona, one I'll never forget.

 albert morgan ⇒

I'm with my wife

Jackie and her friend Kate
Wilson at the after-match party.
We were all on a total high,
but I can't believe
how high I managed to
lift the cup!

⇐ **denis irwin**

Chapter 2

Further Afield

This chapter helps to illustrate why Manchester United are regarded as the world's most widely supported football club. It includes our pre-season tour of Australia, China and Hong Kong, plus the mid-season trip to Tokyo where the lads won yet another trophy, the Inter-Continental Cup. In all of those territories, we found United fans at every turn. Perhaps that's taken for granted now, but I still find it amazing when you travel to the other side of the globe, to be greeted by a sea of red shirts and scarves.

The fans in the Far East were visibly excited to meet players they'd previously only seen on a TV screen or in the pages of a magazine. Some of them may have photographs that I've taken pinned to their bedroom walls, and yet I seemed to pass through airports unnoticed! Not that I envy the players for their fame. Pre-season tours can be hard work, as they take on a tiring schedule of training, playing, signing autographs and making public appearances. Of course, the more active they are on tour, the better it is for me. After all, you can only take so many photographs of hotels and dressing rooms!

I particularly enjoy it when the lads go out and about on excursions to famous landmarks and locations. For example, there's a great picture in this chapter of the backroom boys enjoying an ice cream on Bondi Beach in Sydney, Australia. So you'll see that pre-season tours enable me to take photos away from football, photos that show the players and staff relaxing a little bit and having some fun.

I was grateful to Steve McClaren, the assistant manager, for his co-operation on the tour of Australia and the Far East. In the absence of Sir Alex Ferguson, he did a wonderful job as acting manager. I was particularly impressed with him at the endless press conferences. Steve just took everything in his stride. He also created a great atmosphere for me to work in, even encouraging me to take some of the photographs. Steve also roped me in to run nightly quizzes for the squad; these are now regular fixtures when we're away from home. Some of the staff now call me The Quizmaster! Should the quiz tables ever be turned, I'll go for travel as my specialist subject. After seven years with Manchester United, even my wife is impressed by the expert way in which I fold my shirts and pack a suitcase!

John Peters

left: Crown Towers, team hotel, Melbourne, July 1999.

above Sydney Harbour, July 1999.

right Centre Point Tower, Sydney, July 1999.

left and above left Off to the game and signing autographs along the way, Sydney, July 1999.

right Meal time – the players call it fuel not food.

The backroom staff.

We had some free time on tour in Sydney,
so we took the bus to Bondi Beach.
Someone had the idea of making it look like Blackpool,
so we went down to the seafront
and bought some ice cream!
(left to right: Jimmy Curran, Tony Coton, Steve McClaren,
Albert Morgan, Dr Mike Stone, Rob Swire).

steve mcclaren

"**This was one evening in Australia,**
when a local millionaire, Ronny Rifkin, invited the
players and staff on to his luxury boat.
He provided all the food and entertainment
and we went all the way round Sydney Harbour which,
lit up at night, was a terrific sight.
I'm in the galley here, enjoying a meal with Jordi and Jaap. "

 ⇑ steve mcclaren

right Training in the sun, Sydney, July 1999.

left Young Aussies watching a United
training session.

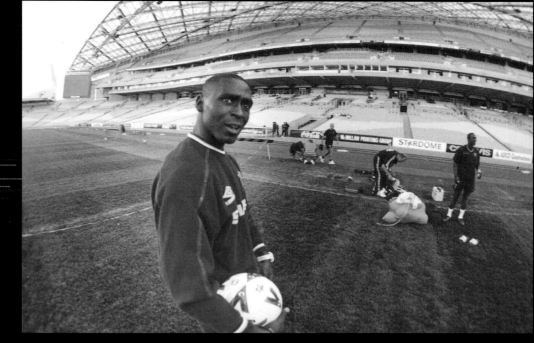

> **I think I'm giving JP** he stick here, winding him up. We're all so used to him now, taking shots of us training that he's just like one of the lads. He's one of us. **"**

andy cole →

> **This is a training** session at the Melbourne Cricket Ground, where we played our first pre-season game. I injured my back on the flight so I was just watching the training... very boring! As usual, John's in my face, following me around. **"**

ole gunnar solskjaer ↑

previous page Training in Sydney, Australia,
July 1999.

> " **This is me telling John to go away!**
> The players always make fun of each other,
> there's always a good atmosphere
> on the bus and around the training ground.
> John fits in well, he's always
> doing quizzes so maybe he's
> asked me a question here that
> I couldn't answer! "

ole gunnar solskjaer

below left Shanghai landscape, July 1999.

below right Red faces, Sydney, July 1999.

above Question time, Shanghai, July 1999.

 When we were in China,
four of the players were asked to visit a school,
as part of the club's project with UNICEF.
I travelled with Phil, Ole, Denis and David
in a minibus, which thankfully was air-conditioned.
It was rather hot outside! ""

↑ **john peters**

right A reflective view of the players at
meal-time, many miles from home.

right Media interest, Hong Kong, July 1999.

below Hong Kong street life.

" **In Hong Kong,**
at the last of the hotels we stayed in
on the long pre-season tour.
That's David May on his way to the
coach for a training session,
flanked by a guard of honour.
The players had similar protection
wherever they went, because
they're hot property in the Far East. "

← **john peters**

" **This is the dressing room,**
before one of the pre-season
games in Australia. The players
on the right have all been named
on the bench. As you can see,
I'm (second from right) not happy
that I'm not playing.
This scene is too familiar! "

← **ole gunnar solskjaer**

left Half-time score, Hong Kong, July 1999.

It looks like I'm holding some ice on Ryan,
during a training session on our pre-season tour.
The pitch was good, but the training on tour was still difficult
because it was very warm and humid.
We lost a lot of fluid, especially in Australia.

 raimond van der gouw

right 'Do You Come From Manchester?',
Hong Kong, July 1999.

below Early arrival, Hong Kong, July 1999.

left Rooftop gardens, Tokyo, November 1999.

below Tokyo cityscape.

"**It is weird when you think**
we've travelled all that way,
to find fans in Malaysia,
in Japan, China and Hong Kong
who adore us.
It's unbelievable how big
Manchester United are over there. "

⇩ `david beckham`

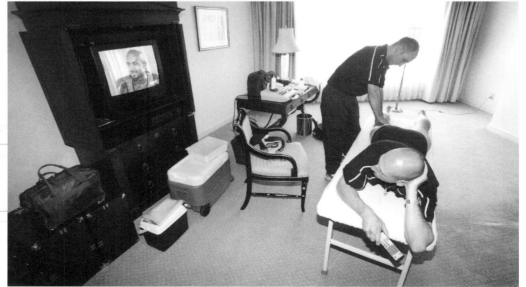

above and next page The players on walk-about in Tokyo, Japan.

"Rob Swire was giving me a massage to loosen my muscles up before the game, so I was watching a little bit of television. It might have been a sports show!"

jaap stam

"
Steve McClaren's
training always varies,
it never gets boring.
It's his way of keeping us
all interested and maintaining
a good team spirit
among the lads.
I'm not bad at this routine,
I'll maybe drop the ball once
on my way across
the pitch. "

← *david beckham*

right Massimo Taibi training in Tokyo.

below Mickael Silvestre, Tokyo, November 1999.

"
Here, John makes me balance
the ball for an hour
while he takes a photograph!
"

paul scholes

above Another training session, this time before the Palmeiras match for the Inter-Continental Cup, November 1999.

> **We've been watching** this goalkeeper for some time now, an Italian named Alberto Morgani, who plays for Cheadle Internazionale. His height might let him down a bit, he's only three foot four. His shot stopping isn't bad but you can only hit soft ones at him. He doesn't talk enough, in fact I've only heard him say, 'Yes, boss'.
>
> **tony coton**

> **Mark Bosnich,** our regular goalkeeper, shows Albert how it should be done. Great save, Bozzie!
>
> **tony coton**

" I'd never seen so many photographers
at one match, when United played
in Tokyo. For the first ten minutes,
there was just a constant din of snapping shutters,
even for something as
uneventful as David Beckham walking towards the corner flag. "

 john peters

"Initially we didn't know how to react after the match in Tokyo.
It was a bit weird because Palmeiras were obviously deeply disappointed about losing.
Then we realized we were World Champions so we really started celebrating!
Funnily enough, we didn't receive any medals for it."

denis irwin

Chapter 3

Home and Away

For all the jet-setting I do with Manchester United, I'll never lose my affection for the bread and butter work in England. I always get a buzz from the home games at Old Trafford, it really is a magnificent stadium and probably the best in the country, facility-wise, for photographers. From the access we're afforded around the pitch, to the purpose-built room under the East Stand, our afternoon or evening's work there is much easier than it is at other Premiership grounds.

As United's club photographer, I have regular duties on the day of a home match. Invariably in this age of success, a presentation is made on the pitch to either a player or the manager, sometimes both. This happens just before kick-off, when I also have to photograph the mascots with the officials and captains in the centre circle. I often almost split myself in two, trying to cover both scenes! I'm on the pitch again at half-time, photographing the lucky winners of the prize draw, and the celebrities who present the cheques. To name-drop just a few in recent seasons, I've photographed Richard Branson, Albert Finney, Angus Deayton and two of the Spice Girls, one of whom has since married David Beckham!

One of the good things about covering away games in England is that I can make a long journey to somewhere like Sunderland, knowing there'll be some familiar faces in the photographers' room when I arrive. The others might work for agencies or for national newspapers but like me, they spend their time following United because of the enormous media interest there is in the club. Before the games we have a cup of tea and a chat about recent photos we've taken – there's plenty of camaraderie. I'm not sure camaraderie is the word to describe my relationship with opposition fans. Sometimes at a smaller ground, I might block someone's view because I sit between them and the action on the pitch. So I've heard all the familiar shouts over the years of 'Who ate all the pies?' or 'Sit down, you fat b....' I've even started a diet on a few occasions!

Words may never hurt me but there was a time when I nearly broke my bones at an away match! I was running towards a good vantage point, when I fell heavily, much to the amusement of about five hundred home fans who were right in front of me. Despite cutting my hands and knees, I managed to regain my composure and got up and took some more photographs for this book. I hope you enjoy them.

John Peters

left: Waiting for kick-off against Omagh Town, August 1999.

> ## This was the hotel
> outside Omagh.
> It was a great game for
> a great cause and I really
> enjoyed it over there.
> As usual in Ireland, we
> were well looked after.

 denis irwin

> ## This is a very moving picture.
> We were in Omagh, pre-season,
> to raise money for the town's
> appeal fund. This young lady
> was guest of honour at a dinner.
> She'd very sadly been blinded by the
> horrific Omagh bomb. She came
> up to meet the manager and
> her favourite player, Andy Cole.
> The manager, as he always
> is on these occasions,
> was lovely with her.

john peters

" It was great for us to be able to go across and do something for the people of Omagh, after the terrible tragedy there. I don't think the game meant so much, but it was just the point of the Manchester United players being there and showing off the cups we'd just won. It was good to lighten their days, just for a moment. **"**

⇩ teddy sheringham

above United XI celebrate one of nine goals against Omagh Town, August 1999, at the benefit match for the victims of the Omagh bombing.

"
I got myself in a bit
of hot water for my response
at Wembley during the Charity Shield
match in August 1999,
to the Arsenal fans giving me stick.
As soon as I started putting
my three fingers up and
pretending to lift trophies,
they seemed to get quite incensed.
The police told me at half-time
to stop it. They said I might
incite a riot. But I did it again
in the League game at Old Trafford,
partly to liven up our supporters
who were a bit quiet while
Arsenal were controlling the game.
I knew that as soon as I
got up off the bench, the Arsenal
fans would absolutely cane me.
But I also knew the United
fans would love it if I showed them
the three fingers. They started
to sing my name, and it livened
the place up. When I returned to
the bench, the other subs
said, 'You loved that, didn't you?'
Damn right I did! "

teddy sheringham

above Wembley re-visited for the Charity Shield against Arsenal, August 1999.

right David Beckham on the opening day of the 1999/2000 season at Goodison Park, August 1999.

“ I think the fans at Old Trafford are very photogenic. From the children with the painted faces to the old fans with their cloth caps, they're all part and parcel of the occasion. This young lad was getting very, very excited and at one stage I had to look for some cotton wool to put in my ears because he was making more noise than the entire West Stand. ”

 john peters

right. Going to plan against Sheffield Wednesday, Old Trafford, August 1999. The match ended 4-0.

right Tango at Highbury. Keane, who scored a
second-half brace, clashes with Patrick Vieira
of Arsenal, August 1999.

"When I'm working at the training ground,
I have one eye looking through the lens and
another eye on players such as David May
who might wallop a football at me. Fortunately in
this photo, David was far too busy
to bother me!"

 john peters

" The press are pictured here, receiving a statement from the club regarding Roy Keane's contract negotiations. At the time, Roy delayed his decision, leaving the press in limbo and the United fans wondering whether their captain would stay or go. The chap handing out the statements is another Roy, Roy Unwin. He's one of the figures of Old Trafford who I see maybe six or seven times a week – he appears everywhere. I'm sure he's got a bed inside the stadium somewhere because he seems to live there! " **john peters** →

" Another press conference at Old Trafford. I think Manchester United have always been aware of their need to cater for vast numbers of photographers and journalists, from England, Europe and around the world. They've always approached it in a professional manner because they have to consider the interests of their sponsors. Sharp, and now Vodafone, obviously want to see their names on television and in magazines and newspapers as often as possible. The club readily caters for the media, even though the media will sometimes have a pop at the players, either individually or collectively. "

← **john peters**

above Reluctant departure. Newcastle's Dabizas is given his marching orders by referee Jeff Winter despite the pleas of Shearer and stand-in manager Steve Clarke as United win 5-1 at Old Trafford, August 1999.

right The final score, Old Trafford.

"**At this press conference,**
the announcement was made that
Manchester United would not
take part in the FA Cup
because of their commitment to the
World Club Tournament in Brazil.
Some strong questions were asked
by the media,
but again Sir Alex Ferguson,
the Chairman and David Davies from
the FA argued the point.
I don't think the manager looked
particularly happy at the time.
I'm sure it was also disappointing for
the fans and the players,
because it was almost an annual
trip to Wembley for us
in the 1990s. "

john peters

above Going for a 'Song' – Dwight Yorke competes with Rigobert Song during United's 3-2 win over Liverpool at Anfield, September 1999.

> **Liverpool 2, United 3.**
> They're always great games
> at Anfield so when you do
> score or set up a goal,
> you have to celebrate
> like this because there's
> so much passion in these games.
> You can tell by my face
> that I enjoyed it.

david beckham

opposite top The fans view against Wimbledon, Old Trafford, September 1999. Yorke leaps away from the challenge of Ben Thatcher as Marcus Gayle looks on.

opposite bottom Ole Gunnar Solskjaer endures a heavy challenge from Wimbledon's Jason Euell, as Phil Neville looks on, Old Trafford, September 1999.

above Thanking the crowd after the Zagreb match at Old Trafford, September 1999.

right Young Reds before the Wimbledon match at Old Trafford, September 1999.

" **I'm used to doing this now.**
It's nice signing for fans because
when I was young I wanted autographs
from the players I loved.
It's good to give a little bit back to
the kids who enjoy watching you play. "

 david beckham

" JP even followed me on to *A Question of Sport*! I've done that twice now, and I really enjoy it. I like Ally McCoist and John Parrot – they make you feel very welcome. We have a good laugh and I enjoy working with them. "

andy cole

left Waiting for goals in the 3-3 draw with
Southampton at Old Trafford, September 1999.

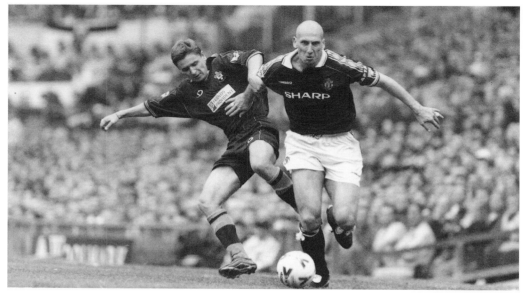

above Too hot to handle. Andy Cole evades Leboeuf and Jes Hogh at Stamford Bridge, October 1999.

left Big Jaap Stam – shrugging aside Marians Pahars of Southampton, Old Trafford, September 1999.

"Losing 5-0 at Chelsea was a very strange feeling. United don't lose very often, but when they do, they seem to get hammered. Four in Barcelona, five at Newcastle, six at Southampton... I don't know why that is. I think I'll stick to photography!

In the second half, it was obvious we were going to lose the game, so I turned the camera away from the pitch and took some photographs of the dug-outs and the crowd. The stony expressions among the United staff tell their own story.

A few years ago, we were beaten 4-0 in Barcelona. Travelling home with the team, I felt quite uncomfortable. I didn't know what to say or where to look. But you cannot win every game, there will always be results which go against you. "

 john peters

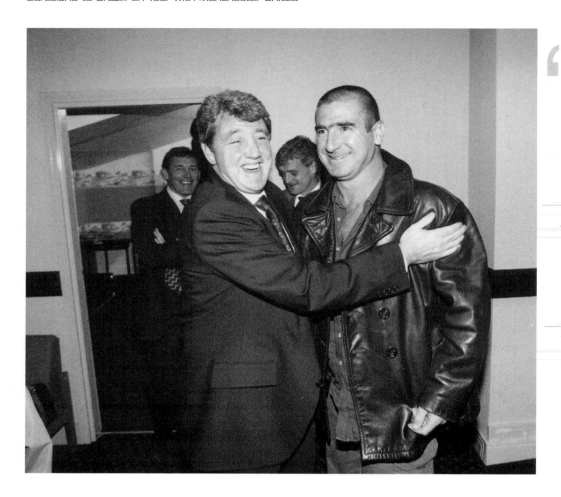

" This was behind the scenes at the manager's testimonial match at Old Trafford in October 1999.
I was privileged to be in the players' lounge as the former players were arriving. Of course, Eric's presence still causes a stir.
If I remember rightly, Steve Bruce was having a crack at Eric's weight! There are four great players in this photo – if you look at the background aswell – and three of them are now in management. "

← **john peters**

" This is in the dressing room after Sir Alex Ferguson's Testimonial.
Taribo asked me to sign his shirt – I think it was for his son.
It's great when even players like Taribo West come up to me, asking me to sign. "

david beckham

"The manager thanked the fans
for their support at the end of his testimonial game.
I was trying to capture him and the crowd
in one photograph, and although we only
see Sir Alex from the back, his posture
speaks volumes. He's in touch with the fans,
he sees things from their viewpoint,
and supports their access to the club
and its players." *john peters*

right Finding open spaces against Watford, Old Trafford, October 1999.

above Mark's return to Villa Park would always be volatile but he took it all in his stride.

" I love pictures like this because it's not just about the bench in the centre of the picture, it's also the fans who make it. All facing the same way, with very similar facial expressions.

I took this from behind the goal, with a 400mm lens and a converter. The manager stands up throughout the game.

On a few occasions, I've taken photographs from the steps below the manager, and discovered that he motions to play every single ball, with his head or his feet. "

john peters

" **The moment I scored**
an own goal at Tottenham.
Not a picture I'd like
a copy of. "

← **paul scholes**

below Tyneside cuisine at a reserve match
against Newcastle, November 1999.

" The best pictures are not always taken at European Cup Finals in Barcelona. This was taken on a cold, wet night at Gigg Lane in Bury. It's a Reserve game against Blackburn and Manchester United were losing 1-0 with about three of four minutes to go when Jonathan Greening fired a shot at goal. I took a picture of the Blackburn goalkeeper making a save. However, the linesman awarded a goal and the goalkeeper was incensed.

He jumped up and ran across to the linesman, aided by one of his defenders, while the United staff watched in the background. The referee came across, had some strong words with the players and then proceeded to send off both the goalkeeper and the defender.

It finished 1-1, and yet, as my picture shows, the ball never went over the line.

I think even the United players were embarrassed to have been awarded that goal. "

john peters

Chapter 4

Europe

Travelling into Europe with Manchester United is like a military manoeuvre. Unlike the lengthy pre-season tours, when the squad has time to relax and sight-see, it's a case on the Continent of flying in, doing a job and then flying out again. The players really only see four things on a European trip – an airport, the inside of a coach, a hotel and a football stadium. Consequently, it didn't seem to matter that we were visiting Croatia for the very first time in October 1999. The very basic facilities at the hotel and football ground reminded us that we were in a relatively poor European country, but other than that, it was hard to form any useful knowledge of life in Zagreb.

It was a different story for me in Graz, a very beautiful city in Austria. On the afternoon of the game while the players slept, I took a taxi ride into the centre with my son Matthew. It was then that I realized the number of times I, like the players, have failed to venture out and really see places on our European travels. It's sad really that the players miss so much, but being cooped up in a hotel has become an accepted part of their job, particularly when the stakes are so great in the Champions League.

United's standards are also high when they're in Europe, so I've been fortunate to stay in some fabulous hotels. Our base in Barcelona was certainly one of the best I've seen, and we were treated to another top place in Marseille. There we stayed in a hotel forty-five minutes from the stadium, in the hills, overlooking a beautiful golf course. But it rained. Heavily. In fact, it hardly stopped from the moment we arrived in Marseille and there was even talk of the game being postponed for twenty-four hours. Fortunately for Phil Morris, the game went ahead as planned. Phil does a wonderful job of organizing the travel, not just for the twenty-plus players but also the coaching staff and the club's media machine.

It pays to be highly organized and self-sufficient when travelling abroad, because we can't take it for granted that we'll be warmly received wherever we go. As a foreign photographer, I've had things thrown at me such as darts and cups of beer. I'll leave you to decide which of those I preferred! Thankfully, crowd trouble has been very rare in my experience of Europe; in fact the only violence you'll see in this chapter is between Nicky Butt and Ryan Giggs, who are really the best of friends!

John Peters

The opening Champions League game
for Season 1999/2000 against NK Croatia
Zagreb at Old Trafford, September 1999.

above First arrival, Monaco, August 1999.

left Coastal view of Monte Carlo, Monaco, August 1999.

" This was a press
conference, held on our arrival
in Monte Carlo for the game
against Lazio. Like all
press conferences, it was all hustle and
bustle, a sea of journalists,
microphones, cameras and
photographers rattling away.
The manager just ploughs on through
them and handles the press in a
remarkable way. "

john peters ⇒

> **This was a special night** for me because we were in Monte Carlo to play in the Super Cup Final in August 1999. The night before the game, I received two European awards, and it was great to be presented them by two of the best players in the world, Johan Cruyff (pictured here) and Michel Platini.

 david beckham ⇒

> **Another sneaky shot** taken on an airport bus. John never stops taking pictures.

⇐ **paul scholes**

"**This was taken during training in** Monte Carlo. The manager has a very good, quite wicked, sense of humour. He certainly makes me laugh! He loves his training sessions, he loves to get involved and have a kick around with the players. He's very fit. One of the things I've seen him do a few times is put a young goalkeeper like Paul Rachubka in the net and he's then taken ten penalties against him. Invariably he scores ten out of ten!" **john peters**

above Media interest focuses on Roy Keane at the Stade Louis II, in Monte Carlo, Monaco, August 1999.

above The Captain's arrival in Austria for the Champions League game against Sturm Graz, September 1999.

left Graz, Austria, September 1999.

> ❝ We're on the coach
> from the airport to the hotel – I can tell that
> because I'm still wearing my suit.
> Most of the time I sit next to Jordi Cruyff or
> on the seat behind him, so I think he was telling
> one of his famous jokes. In Dutch,
> so I had to laugh!
> John surprises me sometimes, because you don't
> always see him taking pictures. It's not one of his
> most beautiful pictures, but it's okay. ❞

jaap stam

"
I'm not sure which airport we're at.
It might be in Austria because they had
billboards in the background.
We have to do a lot of travelling in a season,
and this calls for a lot of patience, especially
when you're waiting for your luggage! "

 jaap stam

above and left: Sampling the surface at the Schwarzenegger Stadium for the match versus Sturm Graz, September 1999.

above Preoccupied fans at the Arnold Schwarzenegger stadium, September 1999.

left Heading for victory against Sturm Graz.

"It's a fun routine that we do in training, the day before a game. They have a laugh, taking the mickey out of any team-mates who get it wrong. As you can see from the photographs, they enjoy it immensely. But they have to keep an alert mind, so it has a benefit. "

 steve mcclaren ⟹

" **I'm trying to find out which players**
aren't concentrating! They line up
in single file, and I stand at the head of the line,
where I give them exercises to do, such as
jumping up and heading
an imaginary ball. "

← steve mcclaren

left Room mates Ryan Giggs and Nicky Butt having fun at training.

above Training at full stretch, Stade Velodrome, October 1999, before the Champions League match against Olympique Marseille.

above 2-1 winners over Olympique Marseille, Old Trafford, September 1999. Cole celebrates after his overhead equalizer.

left Winning numbers against Marseille at Old Trafford, September 1999. Cole and Yorke congratulate Paul Scholes after his late match-winner.

above Room with a view, Marseille, October 1999.

" **This was taken** before the Marseille game in October 1999. I don't think I trained that day because I had a tight hamstring. "

andy cole ⇧

left Henning Berg in the treatment room in Marseille, before the Champions League match, October 1999.

"Here's David Beckham leaving the hotel in Marseille, on his way to the game. He's accompanied as ever by my friend Ned Kelly, who looks after the team's security. Ned has a very busy job looking after them all, but in particular David, in whom there is so much interest from the fans and the media."

john peters →

"It's like this a lot of the time now when we go away. Even in a foreign country, there are fans waiting for us. All the players are good, they all sign autographs and are always polite."

← **david beckham**

above and top Firework display! Marseille,
October 1999.

left All eyes on the game against Olympique
Marseille, October 1999.

Danny Higginbotham, Jonathan Greening and Mark Wilson just beginning, hopefully for them, on the long road to the top at Manchester United.

They're in the first team squad so they travel to a lot of games knowing that there's really little chance of them playing at this stage in their careers. It's all part of their learning curve.

The manager insists that they travel in shirt and tie, looking smart, because they're representing Manchester United. This could almost be a shot from the 1950s... especially with Willo's haircut! **john peters**

 We're on the bus at an airport, but I've really no idea which airport it is! John Peters just snaps away, doesn't he? "

← denis irwin

right: Another press conference, Croatia, October 1999.

" **Like the manager, Roy Keane has**
a very dry, wicked sense of humour.
He's very sharp and quite personal
with it at times. I like this picture because
it's the real Roy. He might wear a stern look most of
the time in public, but to me he's a really
funny bloke! He's a nice family man
who loves his football. "

 john peters ⇒

left Stretching time, Croatia, 1999.

> ## This is Andy and myself in the hotel
> in Florence. I think we were waiting
> to go training, the night before the Fiorentina match.
> We see a lot of hotels – it's part and parcel
> of the game.

↑ **denis irwin**

right Training in Florence. Tony Coton and Mark Bosnich, November 1999.

left Steve McClaren.

" **I'm with Bozzie here,**
having dinner in Florence, though
he's probably eaten all the food.
The talk seems very serious at first,
but in the next photo,
I finally get his joke! "

denis irwin

" **Whenever the players leave the hotel**
there are fans waiting to get autographs.
There are always plenty of teenage girls,
who especially want to meet Ryan Giggs and
David Beckham. But there are also some very grown-up
children who follow Manchester United!
Quite often, a fan will approach a player with a
picture to sign, and when he's done the first one,
he'll find there's another one underneath.
Sometimes there are twenty or thirty pictures
and the player's expected to spend
twenty minutes signing them! "

 john peters

left Morning stroll, Florence, November 1999, before the opening match in the second phase of the Champions League.

"These pictures show the players on their regular morning walk on the day of a game, this time in Florence. It's funny, in a place like this I often wonder what the local people such as the keeper of the shop, think when twenty-two young men walk past wearing tracksuits, followed by photographers. It's a strange scene. And although the players use bikes for exercise at Carrington, I don't think any of them travel home on them these days!"

 john peters ⇒

"This was in Florence again, the day before we played Fiorentina. It was in November so it wasn't too hot over there – that's why I'm wearing a hat. I only took it off for heading practice! I look a bit tired, probably because of all the travelling. **"**

⇓ **jaap stam**

"This was my room in Florence. In our spare time before a game, I like to read a good book. This time it was *The Testament* by John Grisham. I like him. He's a great writer. The books are better than the films though. **"**

⇑ **jaap stam**

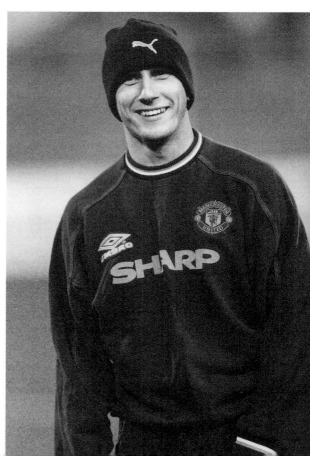

" **This is one of the** routines we do in training, the day before a match. Steve tells us to go left or right, while pointing in the opposite direction. It's all about how quickly you can react to instructions. You have to listen to the shout, not follow his hand.

In the second photograph it looks like Phil Neville's having a nightmare, but in the final one, you'll see it's me who has a hell of a nightmare!

There are no penalties if you get it wrong, but the other lads take the mickey out of you really badly! "

quinton fortune →

" Before each Champions League game,
the two teams line up for the photographers.
Gary Neville is always the first to crouch
down, but he's always the first up.
This upsets a lot of photographers because,
as you can see, he's ruined the shot!
But it's hard to blame the player
– he just wants to get on with the job in hand.
Look out for this when you next see
a European game... I guarantee that every
single time Gary will be the first on his feet,
with a spring in his step. "

 john peters

" **In December 1999,**
I went to Turin with three of the players.
Dwight Yorke, David Beckham and Ole Gunnar
Solskjaer were filming a television commercial
for Pepsi, United's official soft drinks supplier.

We flew out from Biggin Hill airfield in Kent
in a small private jet and then travelled in fast cars
from Turin airport to the Juventus stadium.
The players spent a full day at the stadium
making the commercial, while I took pictures
around it for the club and for Pepsi.
We travelled there and back in a day.

We left Biggin Hill very early in the morning,
about 6.30am and returned the same night,
at about 10pm. Everybody, myself included,
was shattered! "

 john peters

" **The catering at the**
Pepsi shoot in Turin wasn't
really to the lads' liking,
so they had a word in
someone's ear, and sent
out for pizzas. David
asked for pineapple,
but it's not a familiar
ingredient in Italy,
the land of the pizza! "

john peters

above The Pepsi shoot at the Juventus
Stadium, Italy.

Chapter 5

Brazil

The trip to Rio de Janeiro in January 2000 was arguably the best I've been on with Manchester United. The results may not have gone our way, but I thought the tournament in general was a success. I certainly hope we'll take part in the World Club Championships again, whether it's held in Brazil, Japan or at home in England. Photographically, there were some great opportunities for me in Rio, where we enjoyed some fantastic weather. It was also in my favour that we stayed at the same hotel for ten days, because it gave the players a bit of time to see the sights of this amazing city. We had an excellent beach across the road at Sao Conrado, much quieter than the more famous Copacabana and Ipanema.

The squad did sample Copacabana one afternoon. And although it was Sunday, the busiest day of the week, the players managed to mingle quite well with the locals. They even had a game of beach football, and quite a large crowd gathered... probably a bigger crowd than the one which saw United's final game in the Maracana Stadium! The local players were incredibly talented, so our lads felt no shame in losing!

Another crowd gathered high on Rio's Corcovado mountain, when the players and staff went to see the statue of Christ The Redeemer. It's part and parcel of the players' lives but it's a shame if they can't fully relax and enjoy some of the world-famous sights. The swarm of supporters and other tourists also denied me the chance to take an unusual group photograph, with Jesus in the team! Still, I managed to photograph most of the individual players against the backdrop of the statue, primarily for their own personal albums. They didn't so much invite me on that excursion as tell me I was going... with plenty of film! I think they rely on me now to take any photos they might want; very rarely will you see a United player carrying his own camera on tour!

My only dilemma on trips such as the one to Rio is that I can almost have too many opportunities, especially when the squad splits up into small groups. If I decide, for example, to follow Teddy Sheringham and Denis Irwin around the golf course, I might miss David Beckham and Dwight Yorke playing volleyball. Peters the photographer can never be in two places at once, at least not until my son Matthew shares an equal load of the work! But until then, enjoy the photographs taken by yours truly in Brazil, as we round off eight months on the move with Manchester United.

John Peters

" Every day after training in Brazil,
we'd go in the pool. It was the warmest
pool I've ever been in. It was beautiful. Here I'm cheering on
a few of the lads in a swimming race – I think Bozzie won. **"**

 andy cole

Ryan Giggs taking
a shower outdoors after training –
certainly a change from Salford.
When I showed him this
photo, he asked 'Is this a
calendar shot, if so can I
be November?'

john peters →

"Copacabana beach on a Sunday morning. There were probably one hundred thousand people on the beach that day, but somehow David Beckham and Mark Wilson managed to stroll almost unnoticed. On a Sunday morning, I would normally be sat at home in Middleton, reading the papers and drinking coffee. So that was a very different kind of Sunday morning... especially for January!"

 john peters ⇒

> " **I'm on the Copacabana**
> beach here, just waiting for a
> game of head tennis
> against the locals. We took a lot of
> stick in the papers for going to Brazil
> but I'm glad we did. It was
> a good experience. Rio is an amazing place,
> and I'd have no hesitation about going
> back there. I could even play out there.
> For the first two weeks back in
> England, I had to ask myself, 'What am I
> doing here?' After training you go home,
> have a cup of tea and just sit there,
> watching *Fifteen To One* and
> *Countdown* while outside it's pitch black
> and freezing cold. Over there in Brazil,
> the kids are playing floodlit football
> or head tennis on the beach every night
> until eight, nine or ten o'clock, and it's
> beautiful. What a way to live! "

← teddy sheringham

> " **After training sessions**
> the players would relax with
> a game of beach volley ball
> on the beach.
> In this shot Teddy Sheringham
> has just failed to do an
> overhead kick. "

john peters →

This was at Flamengo's
training ground.
There were great facilities there,
and as you can see, I enjoyed
the beach volleyball!

david beckham

Another happy, smiling
Roy Keane, in the pool
after training in Rio.
I think he may have
just won a swimming race.

john peters

"This shot was taken on the players' daily walk. Every morning in Brazil they went for a short walk along the beach. There's sun, sand and local surfers – pretty different from walking down to the training ground at home."

 john peters

In some spare time

during our trip to Brazil, some
of the players and I went off to
Sugar Loaf mountain. While we
were waiting for the cable car
I noticed a huge mirror and
thought it would be interesting
to do a picture with Jaap Stam
and Solskjaer
reflected in it.

john peters

While we were in Brazil

Roy Keane won yet another
award and for the presentation
a live TV satellite link was set
up with RTE in Ireland.
While we were waiting for the link,
the manager, who was
presenting the award, and
Roy started taking the mickey
out of one another and it gave
me another opportunity to
photograph them.

john peters

" **David Beckham** during training at Flamengo's ground with the recently lopped off locks. "

⇓ *john peters*

" **Dwight Yorke showing Brazilian kids** how to do it. We were entertained after training by a group of youngsters who'd made their musical instruments out of tins and bottles. Dwight got into the swing and danced away, to give the press some great pictures. " *john peters* ⇑

“ **Crowd shot of Brazilian** fans. I am always on the look out for great shots of fans and this guy with a painted face who was balancing quite precariously on the stand, really stood out. ”

← *john peters*

“ **The first game in Rio,** against Necaxa of Mexico, and sadly David was sent off.
One of the opposition players seemed to run across and grab David by the hair pulling him back.
That went almost unmentioned, anywhere.
I watched this through a long lens and I felt that the other guy would surely be booked for retaliation. But the referee did nothing to him.
Funnily enough, Necaxa stayed in the same hotel as us, but there were no fisticuffs in the foyer! ”

john peters →

"**Tuesday 11 January 2000.**
Although the Maracana Stadium filled up for the second game that evening,
which featured the local Vasco de Gama team, the crowd was
very small for the first match of the evening between
Manchester United and South Melbourne. This is one of my favourite pictures,
showing a scene from that game, when there were
more people on the United bench than in the
crowd behind them."

 john peters